BOOK ANALYSIS

Written by Anne Delandmeter
Translated by Rose Brichard

AF143853

The Ladies' Paradise

BY ÉMILE ZOLA

Bright
≡Summaries.com

ÉMILE ZOLA

FRENCH WRITER AND JOURNALIST

- **Born in Paris in 1840**
- **Died in Paris in 1902**
- **Notable works:**
  - *Nana* (1880), novel
  - *The Ladies' Paradise* (1883), novel
  - *Germinal* (1885), novel

Born in 1840, Émile Zola is one of the most celebrated novelists of 19th century France. He died in 1902, and is renowned as the pioneer of naturalism, a literary movement which expressed the new scientific innovations of the time in literary form, grounded in detail and real observation. In his novels, Zola works around a hypothesis which he proves through literary experimentation. Zola's most notable literary output is his *Rougon-Macquart* cycle of novels, which illustrate his literary philosophy and aesthetic. This series of twenty books was hugely successful despite its many critics.

Zola is also famous for his political standpoints, through which he often publicly denounced the workings of the world around him. This is most visible in his condemnation of the Dreyfus affair. In response to this military and political scandal in France, Zola wrote a public letter entitled *J'accuse…!* (1898) which largely contributed to the resolution of the affair and Captain Dreyfus being cleared of the charges levelled against him.

THE LADIES' PARADISE

A STORY OF CAPITALISM'S TRIUMPH

- **Genre:** novel
- **Reference edition:** Zola, E. (1886) The Ladies' Paradise. [online]. Trans. Vizetelly, E. A., London: Vizetelly & Co. [Accessed 13th July 2016]. Available from: <http://gutenberg.net.au/ebooks14/1400561h.html>
- **First edition:** 1883
- **Themes:** naturalism, success, capitalism, industrialisation, trade

The Ladies' Paradise ("*Au Bonheur des Dames*" in the French), is part of a series of twenty novels known as the *Rougon-Macquart*. Zola's novel cycle is subtitled *The natural and social history of a family under the Second Empire* ("*Histoire naturelle et sociale d'une famille sous le second Empire*"). This work traces a family as it climbs the social ladder after Napoleon III's coup d'état in 1851 where he declared himself emperor of France. These novels were written between 1871 and 1893, and include other notable works such as *L'Assommoir, Nana* and *Germinal*. The novels can be read independently of each other and in whichever order the reader chooses.

The Ladies' Paradise is the eleventh work in the series, and tells the story of how a new department store threatens the survival of smaller businesses in the area. Alongside this, Zola also tells a love story between the department store's owner Octave Mouret, a character from the novel's prequel

Pot-Bouille (1882), and a saleswoman named Denise. The novel was well-received when it was first published in 1883.

SUMMARY

CHAPTER 1

After her parents' death, a 20-year-old woman called Denise goes with her two brothers to stay with her Uncle Baudu in Paris. She is attracted by the apparent luxury of the department store - The Ladies' Paradise - across the road. Her uncle is unable to accommodate Denise as planned, and she discovers that the womenswear department at The Ladies' Paradise is hiring. She decides to go there the following day to express her interest despite her uncle's loud protests against the "bazaar" which is slowly drawing customers away from all the other shops in the area.

CHAPTER 2

Denise arrives at The Ladies' Paradise at the same time as Deloche, a young man who is just as shy as she is. No-one sees any potential in Denise except Mouret, the owner of the whole shop, who intervenes before she is sent away and speaks of Denise's "hidden charm". Denise thinks she has fallen in love with a salesman named Hutin.

CHAPTER 3

Mouret's lover Madame Desforges invites Baron Hartmann, director of *Crédit Immobilier*, Mouret, and other bourgeois notables to tea on Saturday. Mouret is very popular among this crowd who have all been seduced by the glamour of The Ladies' Paradise. He is trying to convince the baron to give up some buildings to allow him to expand his shop further. Baron Hartmann agrees to this on the condition that the sale planned for the following Monday is as successful as Mouret claims it will be.

CHAPTER 4

Denise starts work the day the new winter lines go on sale. The other saleswomen are not impressed by the new addition, and ensure that she handles no important sales. Meanwhile, the salesmen are all in competition with each other to find the customer who is willing to spend the most. The crowds begin flowing in the afternoon and The Ladies' Paradise takes "the highest [sales] figure ever attained in one day".

CHAPTER 5

Denise has made it through her first two months, despite being exhausted and still disliked by her womenswear colleagues. Her only friend, Pauline, tells her that she should find a lover to help her make it through. One day, Denise bumps into Hutin with another girl outside Paris; she is crestfallen. The same day, Deloche admits that he is in love with her, but she does not reciprocate his feelings. She is on her way back home when she walks right into Mouret, who also finds himself somewhat agitated in Denise's presence.

CHAPTER 6

When summer - the quietest time of year for The Ladies'

Paradise - arrives there is panic at the shop. Many employees are dismissed and rumours about Denise begin circulating - people think that one of her brothers is her lover and that the other is her son. Hutin starts being rude to her and Mouret finds out that Denise is working nights to earn extra money. Bourdoncle, who is in charge of general control and surveillance at The Ladies' Paradise - wants to dismiss Denise, but once again Mouret insists that she stay. Just after this, Denise is speaking to the brother everyone believes to be her lover in the corner of the shop. Bourdoncle dismisses her for her actions. Mouret learns that this was in fact her brother and is furious that he was not consulted on the matter.

CHAPTER 7

Demise sub-lets a room from Bourras, one of the small business-owners in the area, who takes her in out of pity. She finds a new job as a saleswoman in Robineau's silk shop not far from The Ladies' Paradise. Robineau is being forced to lower his prices to compete with the department store, and a price war between the two businesses begins. Inevitably, Robineau loses, unable to lower his prices further. Denise bumps into Mouret in the street. He apologises for the misunderstanding which caused her dismissal.

CHAPTER 8

A new street is built, called the Rue du Dix-Decembre, to house the expanding department store and construction on The Ladies' Paradise continues day and night. Baudu's daughter Geneviève discovers that her fiancé Colomban is in love with a Ladies' Paradise saleswoman named Clara. She is heartbroken. Denise realises that Robineau no longer has the means to pay her wages but is afraid to dismiss her. She therefore returns to The Ladies' Paradise and learns that Clara has slept with Mouret, a man who triggers feelings of "unknown uneasiness" in Denise. She tells Colomban the news.

CHAPTER 9

During the "great exhibition of summer novelties", Mouret puts his new ideas for driving up sales into practice. He uses advertising, quickly restocks products, deliberately makes it look as though there are crowds of people in the shop with everything in disorder, and introduces a returns policy which allows the customer to bring back goods they are not satisfied with. Denise is finally accepted into the folds of the womenswear team.

Madame Desforges is jealous of Clara's affair with Mouret, and comes to the shop to see her. Instead, she discovers her true rival, the woman Mouret can't take his eyes off of: Denise. Mouret promotes Denise to second in department and realises he has feelings for her. She too is carrying a torch for him, but feels humiliated and hurt when he offers her money.

CHAPTER 10

Denise is now better-off financially and truly at home in her job; she has "conquered the department". Mouret sends her a letter inviting her to dine with him at his house. Everyone begins speaking about her behind her back, and rumours that she got her promotion by sleeping with the boss begin circulating. Mouret meets with Denise and declares his love for her. He begs her to dine with him, to which she replies, "I am not a Clara, to be thrown over in a day. Besides, you love another; yes, that lady who comes here. Stay with her. I do not accept half an affection."

CHAPTER 11

Madame Desforges hatches a plan to humiliate Denise by inviting both her and Mouret to her house at the same time, under the pretence that she needs Denise to come and touch up a newly-bought coat. Mouret accepts her invitation in the hope of meeting Baron Hartmann to discuss a business matter. Madame Desforges asks him to join her in her bedroom so Denise will be forced to confront him, feeling "delighted to lower the young girl to this servant's work". She talks down to Denise, but Mouret defends her.

CHAPTER 12

Finally, "Denise's reign was commencing". Everyone respects her, though there are still rumours that she has had some sort of affair with Deloche. Mouret is more and more troubled by Denise's rejection. The Ladies' Paradise expands yet again, to the extent that the "staff would now have sufficed to people a small town".

Mouret finds Denise and Deloche together and believes that they must be lovers. He begs Denise to explain herself, but she refuses. Mouret promotes her yet again to the head of the children's clothing department. Pauline tells Denise that everyone thinks she is only resisting Mouret's advances to try and make him marry her. She decides to leave The Ladies' Paradise.

CHAPTER 13

Geneviève takes ill and dies after being abandoned by Colomban. Her funeral seems to almost be a protest against The Ladies' Paradise. Robineau attempts suicide, Madame Baudu dies of a broken heart, Bourras is evicted from his premises, and Baudu shuts down his shop. Despite all these misfortunes, Denis thinks "that all this misery [is]... necessary for the health of the Paris of the future". She finds that she is more in love with Mouret than ever.

CHAPTER 14

On the day the "grand exhibition of white goods" opens, The Ladies Paradise draws enormous crowds. Mouret thinks that Denise left her job for a lover, when in fact she is taking refuge in Valognes to escape all the rumours about her.

Though Mouret believes that remarrying will be bad luck for the shop ("the introduction of a woman changed the air, drove away the others, by bringing her own odor"), he nevertheless proposes to Denise. She tells him that she loves him but leaves for Valognes. He comes to find her to "bring her back, all-powerful, and his wedded wife".

CHARACTER STUDY

DENISE BAUDU

Denise is the protagonist of the novel, and all the other characters are defined in relation to her. Orphaned, she is a simple country girl who arrives in Paris with her two brothers at her side. She is almost like a mother towards them, sacrificing everything. Penniless, she goes to Paris in the hope that her uncle will take them in, but he is unable to. She needs a way to make money, and begins working at Mouret's department store. She is virtuous and has a strong moral compass, refusing to be anyone's lover, despite everyone telling her that "a woman always needs a man" (Chapter 1).

Throughout the novel, Denise's character undergoes a true evolution:

- Physically: Denise is initially described as sickly-looking with badly-cut thick blonde hair and a sad face. She is known as "the unkempt girl" (Chapter 5) among the staff, yet as the novel progresses, it seems everyone finds her increasingly attractive and charming;
- As the story moves on, Denise's standard of living and her status improve. She goes from being just a saleswoman right up to head of department. From the outset, she feels confident about her future.

At the beginning of the novel, Denise thinks she is in love with Hutin, a fellow salesman, but finds herself somewhat uneasy whenever she is near Mouret. Eventually she realises that she is in love with her boss. However, she is happy to be alone and has no desire to marry. This quotation - "It was by a sort of instinct of happiness that she still remained so obstinate, to satisfy her need of a quiet life, and not from any idea of virtue." (Chapter 12) - shows her to be largely liberated from the social norms of the day in her thinking, and thus she comes to represent a woman striking back against society. Several people warn Mouret about the danger this vengeance presents, for example, he is told that women "draw more blood and money from you than you have ever sucked from them" (Chapter 11). However, Mouret can't tempt Denise into a relationship, despite his great fortune, and suffers greatly because of this. It is impossible to put a price on love, and all the money in the world can't buy him the woman he wants.

Denise lives in two parallel worlds. She experiences the new frontiers of the modern world, sharing Mouret's ideas and opinions about business and capitalism. At the same time, she also lives in a very traditional sphere, as she is closest to the small business owners. She is full of compassion regarding their deteriorating situation, yet she can't help but see change in a positive light. She even improves business for Mouret and encourages him to take action to ensure better working conditions for the staff.

OCTAVE MOURET

In the past, Mouret had "suddenly and mysteriously made the conquest of Madame Hédouin, who brought him The

Ladies' Paradise as a marriage portion" (Chapter 1). He seduces Madame Desforges so he can make a connection with one of her lovers - Baron Hartmann.

He is a flirtatious and seductive character, extremely sure of himself, and full of optimism and passion ("I would rather die of passion than boredom!" - Chapter 11). He considers women as useless and superficial beings, just another object used to maximise profit; all that changes when he meets Denise and falls madly in love.

Figures not dissimilar to Mouret - someone who will stop at nothing to achieve greatness - appear in various forms throughout the *Rougon-Macquart* series. In Mouret's case, he wants his business to achieve its maximum potential, with a strong desire to improve the inner functions and systems of the machine that is The Ladies' Paradise.

THE LOCAL SHOPKEEPERS

The local shopkeepers come together to form opposition to the department store, and slowly die off one by one in the battle against The Ladies' Paradise; eventually, they all fall victim to this new vision of capitalism. Denise tries to persuade them to sell their businesses to Mouret's department store on several occasions, but they all refuse the offer. Yet it is clear that Denise depends on these people; she arrived at her Uncle Baudu's seeking shelter, then she begins working for Bourras, who employs her to help her out even though he hardly has the means to pay her wages, and finally she works for Robineau before returning to The Ladies' Paradise.

As the department store continues to expand, the situation only worsens for the local businesses. The Baudu family is a perfect example of this deterioration. Their daughter Geneviève dies, after her fiancé abandons her for a saleswoman he would never have met were it not for The Ladies' Paradise. Monsieur Baudu's wife dies of a broken heart not long after her daughter, and when the shopkeepers come to Geneviève's funeral, Denise talks of "the tramping of a flock of sheep led to the slaughter-house, the discomfiture of the shops of a whole district, the small traders dragging along their ruin" (Chapter 13).

THE CUSTOMERS

Madame Henriette Desforges

Madame Desforges is a rich widow who is having a secret affair with Baron Hartmann, a man who has always been her adviser. The baron is aware that she has other lovers and is content with the situation. She is madly in love with Mouret. In his writing, Zola emphasises how jealous she is of Mouret's love for Denise. She is an elegant bourgeois lady, and also visits The Ladies' Paradise to make her own purchases.

Other customers

Each of the shop's customers can be aligned with a certain stereotype; the window-shopper, the customer who buys everything, the thief, etc. All of these are superficial characters whose conversations and thoughts are voiced only in relation to The Ladies' Paradise and its wares. They in some way align with Mouret's negative conception of women and the type of person from which he can generate profit. He believes that women cannot resist a bargain and will buy goods they have no need for just for the sake of it. These customers are enchanted by Mouret, who flatters them constantly, manipulates them, and readies them to enter into his machine made for "devouring the women" (Chapter 3). This idea is further cemented here: "Mouret's unique passion was to conquer woman. He wished her to be queen in his house, and he had built this temple to get her completely at his mercy" (Chapter 8).

ANALYSIS

NATURALISM AND THE PROBLEM OF WRITING TEXTS WHICH ARE TRUE TO LIFE

The triumph of science to come could be sensed everywhere in the air in Zola's era. He encoded science and this new wave into his own writing to endow his novels with a new level of legitimacy; he considered literature to be as scientific as any other field. He was the pioneer of the naturalist movement in French literature, and is considered to be both observing and experimenting in his work. He took time to study the phenomena influencing people of his day, such as inheritance and the social sphere.

In this way, Zola plays with *vraisemblance*, the idea that the image produced is true to life. In his work, he portrays the realities of his time - a time in which trade was booming and industrialisation was in full bloom. He documented, observed and interviewed staff in department stores to add elements of real life into his story.

Zola's use and style of description are also of key importance. *The Ladies' Paradise* is punctuated by several passage of long and careful description, which begin with broader, more general aspects of the situation before plunging into great detail, with regards to colour for example. These passages appear at various points throughout the work, so the reader is never faced with a whole chapter of such saturated writing that describes all of The Ladies' Paradise characteristics in one go. Such details serve to consolidate meaning and representation in the text. As the novel progresses, the descriptions change to reflect the department store's growing success. These not only allow Zola to paint a colourful picture of his own society, but subtly warn the reader against the traps and temptations of department stores, by detailing the tactics they use to entice.

AN OPTIMISTIC NOVEL

This novel, with its overall optimistic tone, breaks away from the norms established by Zola himself in the dark writing he had produced up until that point. *The Ladies' Paradise* may in fact be considered Zola's only optimistic piece of writing. Zola actually wrote the book at a time of great personal difficulty, and wrote the text hoping to rid himself of his sadness and get better.

The novel is a success story for Denise, Mouret and The Ladies' Paradise. Despite the slow death of the surrounding businesses, this new age of the department store is, generally, portrayed as something beneficial for society as a whole. Furthermore, both Denise and Mouret offer to help the local tradesmen out of their financial situation either by trying to buy their businesses for the department store or by offering them jobs in The Ladies' Paradise; it is the business-owners who refuse these offers. There is a truly happy ending, with the two heroes soon to be married.

Zola's desire to create a more light-hearted piece of work is linked to this novel's target audience. In essence, the book was written for a feminine target market, and Zola believed that women preferred happy endings. From this angle, it is almost ironic that Zola appears to share characteristics with Mouret - they both think they understand all aspects of a woman's mindset. Therefore, Zola seeks in some way to indulge his audience; flatter, seduce, and make the sale.

DEPARTMENT STORES AND CAPITALISM

In *The Ladies' Paradise*, Zola describes the evolution of the era in which he himself lived, as industrialisation took on its full force. He had experienced this monumental change, having worked at Hachette, a publishing house which produced a new affordable collection called the *Bibliothèque de gare*, which considerably expanded its readership and market. At this time, literature was becoming a product to sell and circulate in society like all the others, in the same profound state of flux as the money it generated.

While Zola took great care to conduct proper research for this novel, not all the descriptions should be considered realistic. He used the Parisian department store Bon Marché and the Louvre as inspiration for The Ladies' Paradise. This new type of shop appeared on the scene around 1820. Initially, small businesses happily existed alongside these new all-encompassing retail outlets. In *The Ladies' Paradise*, all the local shops disappear within four years, when in reality this kind of transition took around twenty years. However, the ideas Mouret expresses in Chapter Nine do reflect real life. He uses new sales techniques which are part of the developing capitalist system of the time, such as rapid sales and purchases, advertising, having sales staff work on commission on top of their salary, the importance of banks, and the returns system.

The department store, portrayed by Zola as a positive step forward, served to democratise luxury. It can be considered as the "embryo of the vast trades' unions of the twentieth century" (Chapter 12). Its sales systems contrast with those of small businesses, who believe that "The art [of trade] was not to sell a large quantity, but to sell dear" (Chapter 1). These little shops are quickly gobbled up by The Ladies' Paradise, and their owners believe that this new "ogre" (Chapter 14) is compromising the dignity of trade itself. The department store radically changed what it meant to work in retail. Employees lived in bad conditions, and were mere cogs in the "giant machine" (Chapter 10). They only became truly human outside of working life, where they could have relationships and a family.

As the novel progresses, the local shops are increasingly described as dark or cold, conjuring up images of basements and prisons. The Ladies' Paradise on the other hand is described in an ever more positive light: colourful, modern, impressive, and full of life. It can be viewed as the new temple of an increasingly godless modern society. This comparison with religion is expressed directly by Zola: "Women now came and spent their leisure time in his establishment, the shivering and anxious hours they formerly passed in churches" (Chapter 14).

OPPOSITION AND DARWINISM

In many of his books, Zola creates oppositions between different institutions which have contrasting characters. In this work, he sets up a dual opposition between the small shops and the department store, and between the local businessmen (including Baudu) and Mouret as they fight for customers and footfall.

Further conflicts appear within these two worlds.

- A contrast emerges between Mouret and Vallagnosc, his former partner who has a more pessimistic worldview, speaking of misery, mediocrity and the uselessness of all existence. Mouret on the other hand tells him, "What? Do I enjoy myself? What are you talking about? Why, of course I do, my boy, and even when things give way, for then I am furious at hearing them cracking, I am a passionate fellow myself, and don't take life quietly; that's what interests me in it perhaps." (Chapter 2).
- There is fierce rivalry between the different departments, sales staff and customers within the business itself;
- Each of these worlds is represented by a woman. Denise - a poor, sickly, unkempt young woman who knows the value of hard work - is juxtaposed with Madame Desforges, a distinguished lady who lives a life of luxury.

In the work, Zola can be seen to make literary allusion to the idea of natural selection as expressed by Charles Darwin (English biologist and naturalist, 1809-1882) in his *On the Origin of Species* (1859). The earth is a playing field for the survival of the fittest; the least adaptable species (represented by the local businesses) are the first to go extinct. This understanding that extinction is part of the process of evolution colours Denise's outlook; while she feels sorry for her business-owning friends and family, she still feels "that all this misery was necessary for the health of the Paris of the future" (Chapter 13).

FURTHER REFLECTION

SOME QUESTIONS TO THINK ABOUT...

- Compare today's society with the society Zola describes in the novel.
- In what ways is this novel optimistic?
- Compare the rise of the prostitute Nana, the heroine of Zola's novel of the same name, with that of Denise. Use this extract from *Nana* to help: "She has shot up to womanhood in the slums and on the pavements of Paris, and tall, handsome and as superbly grown as a dunghill plant, she avenges the beggars and outcasts of whom she is the ultimate product. With her the rottenness that is allowed to ferment among the populace is carried upward and rots the aristocracy."
- Explain why Zola can be considered as a modern author.
- What is naturalism? Why is Zola called a naturalist?
- How does the novel portray women?
- How does Zola add an illusion of reality to his novel?
- "They were all nothing but the wheels, turned round by the immense machine, abdicating their personalities, simply contributing their strength to this commonplace, powerful total" (Chapter 5). Discuss.
- Describe and discuss examples of how Zola uses contrast and oppositions in *The Ladies' Paradise*.
- What does this quotation say about women, or about people more generally? - "Women now came and spent their leisure time in his establishment, the shivering and anxious hours they formerly passed in churches: a necessary consumption of nervous passion, a growing struggle

of the god of dress against the husband, the incessantly renewed religion of the body with the divine future of beauty" (Chapter 14).

We want to hear from you!
Leave a comment on your online library
and share your favourite books on social media!

FURTHER READING

REFERENCE EDITION

- Zola, E. (1886) *The Ladies' Paradise*. [online]. Trans. Vizetelly, E.A., London: Vizetelly & Co. [Accessed 13th July 2016]. Available from: <http://gutenberg.net.au/ebooks14/1400561h.html>

REFERENCE LITERARY STUDIES

- Adam-Maillet, M. (2000) *Étude sur Zola et le roman*. Paris: Ellipses.
- Belgrand, A. (2000) *Étude sur Émile Zola : Au Bonheur des Dames*. Paris: Ellipses.

ADAPTATIONS

- *Au Bonheur des Dames*. (1930) [film]. Julien Duvivier. dir. France: Le Film d'Art.
- *Au Bonheur des Dames*. (1943) [film]. André Cayatte. dir. France: Continental-Films.

The Paradise. (2012) [Television series]. David Drury, Marc Jobst et al. Dirs. UK: BBC Productions and Masterpiece.

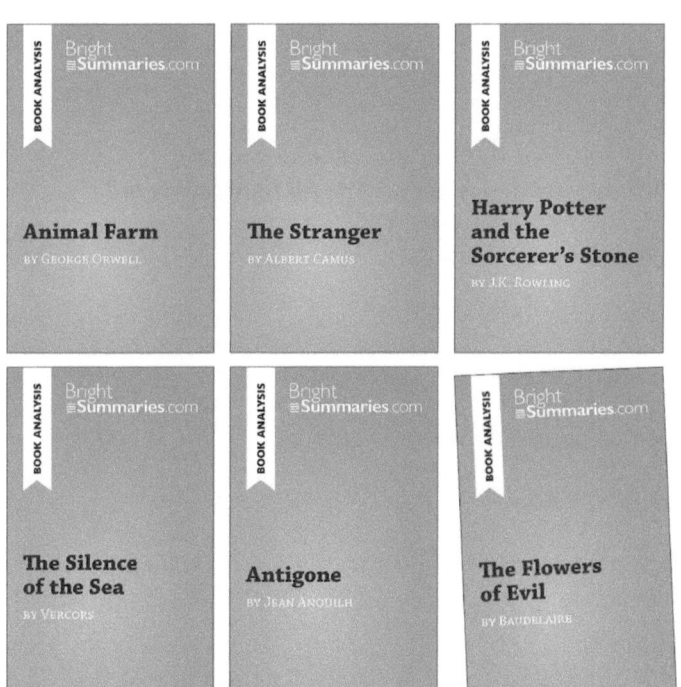

www.brightsummaries.com

Ebook EAN: 9782806280336

Paperback EAN: 9782806282897

Legal Deposit: D/2016/12603/288

Cover: © Primento

Digital conception by Primento, the digital partner of publishers.